5 MINUTE HISTORY

5 MINUTE HISTORY

SCOTT ADDINGTON

FIRST WORLD WAR
GREAT
BATTLES

The History Press

First published 2014

The History Press
The Mill, Brimscombe Port
Stroud, Gloucestershire, GL5 2QG
www.thehistorypress.co.uk

British Library Cataloguing in Publication Data.
A catalogue record for this book is available from the British Library.

ISBN 978 0 7524 9321 3

Typesetting and origination by The History Press
Printed in Europe

CONTENTS

INTRODUCTION

THE FIRST WORLD War lasted for four years, four months and fourteen days, and accounted for over 35 million casualties, almost half of which died; indeed, 230 soldiers perished every hour of the conflict over those four-and-a-bit years. The attrition rate was, and still is, truly astounding.

For a soldier in the front-line trenches, there was a continual fight with the enemy, even if there was no official battle or 'big push' raging. Trench raids, snipers, grenades and, of course, the shelling from enemy artillery caused front-line soldiers on both sides to be in almost constant danger. If this wasn't enough, on top of these daily terrors there were numerous large-scale offensives that have gone down in history as some of the most destructive and bloodiest battles ever waged.

As well as the huge loss of life, these battles are important due to their use of new technology. This was a time when the science of warfare was developing fast; poison gas, underground mines, grenades, mobile flame-throwers, tanks, advances in artillery tactics and the use of the air force for integrated air and ground offensives were all refined on the battlefields of the First World War. It was also when warfare reached beyond the professional soldier. Millions of ordinary men from all over Europe signed up to fight for their country. Even today the newspapers and online communities are full of newly discovered family heroes and their stories, and more often than not, this story involves one of the major battles such as Mons, Loos, the Somme or Passchendaele.

In trying to describe these battles for this *5 Minute History* I have tried to be as succinct as possible without losing sight of the main points for the reader. I have also included a few interesting facts to add a bit of context, plus, with the inclusion of several eyewitness accounts, I have tried to inject a personal touch to these enormous battles. These are particularly fascinating and I have been moved when piecing them all together!

I hope you enjoy this brief overview of some of the most pivotal battles of the First World War and I hope it inspires you to read some of the brilliant in-depth accounts of these clashes that can be found both online and in physical bookshops.

SMA
Spring 2014

MONS

JUST A MATTER of weeks after declaring war on Germany, 80,000 members of the British Expeditionary Force (BEF) along with 30,000 horses and 315 guns of assorted size and calibre had landed in France and were marching straight towards the enemy who were passing through Belgium on their way to Paris.

It was on 22 August 1914 that the British got their first glimpse of a German soldier. During a routine reconnaissance patrol four enemy cavalrymen of the 2nd Cuirassiers were spotted by a forward patrol of the 4th Royal Irish Dragoon Guards, who immediately gave chase and opened fire. Captain Hornby of 1st Troop led his men in the pursuit and charged the Germans, killing several. He returned with his sword presented, revealing German blood.

Meanwhile, to the rear, the rest of the British Expeditionary Force decided to entrench roughly along a loose line at the Mons-Conde canal. They didn't really know how many Germans were on the other side of

DID YOU KNOW?

Four Victoria Crosses were won during the first day of fighting at Mons. They were awarded to Lieutenant M.J. Dease, Private S.F. Godley, Captain T. Wright and Corporal C.A. Jarvis.

I WAS THERE

Our first battle is a heavy, unheard of heavy, defeat, and against the English – the English we had laughed at.

Walter Bloem, Reserve Captain, 12th Brandenburg Grenadier Regiment[1]

DID YOU KNOW?

The British Expeditionary Force consisted of highly trained soldiers and during the battle they maintained such a high rate of fire with their rifles that the German attackers were convinced they were facing machine guns.

the waterway, but they would find out soon enough. Less than 80,000 British troops with 300-odd pieces of artillery were about to face off against 160,000 German soldiers who were backed up by double the amount of artillery.

The German artillery opened up at dawn on 23 August 1914, with the first infantry attack commencing at 9 a.m. Their objective was to take control of the bridges that crossed the canal, and once in possession of these bridges they would then push on directly to the British lines and beyond. They advanced across open country in close formation, making a perfect target for the trained British riflemen. Not surprisingly, they suffered terribly, and by noon they had made little progress despite German bodies piling up.

I WAS THERE

Every house where British could be concealed, every possible observation post, every foot of trench, every hill-crest and 400 yards behind it was swept and devastated by the tornado ... Now battalions and batteries found themselves cut off from their neighbours, each fighting and carrying on by itself. Chetwode's Cavalry Brigade was caught in the thick of it. The Guards held on almost by their teeth. The cavalry had to go; and the Munsters and Black Watch lost horribly as they covered the retirement.

Major A. Corbett Smith, Royal Field Artillery [2]

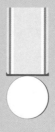

The war was most definitely on.

However, during this time the British Expeditionary Force were being shelled constantly by the massed German artillery and enjoyed little or no cover. Despite this, they held on for six hours before blowing the bridges over the canal and retreating to a pre-established second line position a few miles away. The Germans were tired and disorganised and failed to press home any advantage despite their huge numerical superiority. German reserves were called up and massed for a new attack in the evening. It was here that the British commanders finally realised the size of the enemy, and promptly ordered the retreat.

They had already lost 1,600 men and didn't want to lose too many more. The men were organised, rounded up and the order was given: a fighting retreat towards Maubeuge and then down the road from Bavai to Le Cateau, almost 20 miles away.

THE FIRST BATTLE OF THE MARNE

DESPITE THE SETBACK at Mons, the Germans had steamrollered through northern France in August and September 1914. It seemed to the Kaiser that war was as good as won. He sent medals and congratulatory telegrams to his senior officers, but deep down most of them were worried about the current situation. The careful timing of the Schlieffen Plan had been thrown out of the window, and after advancing more than 300 miles in a month, the troops were on their last legs and supplies were stretched to the limit.

The Allies were also feeling the pace after enduring more than ten days' continual retreat under constant attack from the German guns. They eventually reached a line of relative safety approximately 40 miles south of the River Marne, where they finally got a bit of rest. It would be the calm before the storm.

DID YOU KNOW?

The First Battle of the Marne was a significant victory for the Allies as it destroyed the German plan to invade Paris. However, this battle signalled the end of the mobile war and the beginning of the trench warfare that is so synonymous with the First World War.

I WAS THERE

We rose from cover and doubled forward over the grass … With a sinking heart I realised that our extended line made an excellent target, as we topped a slight rise and went on fully exposed across flat country without the slightest cover. The Germans were waiting for us, holding fire.

As we cleared the crest a murderous hail of missiles raked us from an invisible enemy. The line staggered under this smash of machine gun, rifle and shell fire, and I would say that fully half our men fell over forward onto their faces, either killed or wounded.

Corporal John F. Lucy, Royal Irish Rifles[3]

I WAS THERE

We went forward as we had been trained – one section would advance under covering fire of another section, leapfrogging each other as the others were firing to keep Jerry's head down. My company was going in with their bayonets when suddenly Jerry put up a white flag. We were really surprised. We took 450 prisoners. I said to one of them, 'Why did you pack up when you've got so much ammunition?' He said, 'Well, your fire was so accurate we couldn't put our heads up to shoot you.'

Sergeant Thomas Painting, 1st Battalion, King's Royal Rifle Corps*

20

DID YOU KNOW?

Total casualties for both sides totalled over 500,000. France and Germany both suffered losses in the region of 250,000, with the British Expeditionary Force losing 12,733 men.

After a scuffle at Guise, where the French won a tactical victory, von Bulow, the German Second Army commander panicked a little and asked von Kluck and his First Army for help. Halting his march to the south-west, von Kluck turned his army east, towards Paris itself. This move closed the gap between the two German forces and brought von Kluck to the River Marne, some 30 miles east of Paris, by 3 September.

French air reconnaissance discovered this turn and the infantry quickly prepared for a counter-attack. On the morning of 6 September, the French Sixth Army, under direction from General Joffre, attacked the German First Army flank, achieving complete surprise.

Realising their situation, the Germans had no choice but to withdraw to the north. Between 10 and 12 September they conducted a fighting retreat covering around 40 miles of ground until they established a new line on high ground beyond the River Aisne, destroying everything as they went in an effort to slow the Allied pursuit.

Despite their best efforts, the Allies were unable to finish the Germans off. The chasing soldiers were themselves exhausted; they had run out of shells, too, and to make matters worse the Germans had dug in on high ground which offered good defensive positions. The First Battle of the Marne was over. The Germans had been stopped, but at a cost. Almost 265,000 Allied soldiers were killed, wounded or taken prisoner during this first major battle of the war. A war, it was clear, which would definitely not be over by Christmas.

THE BATTLE OF TANNENBERG

WHEN THE RUSSIANS deployed two armies in August 1914 for the invasion of East Prussia, Germany readied herself for a nightmare scenario: a war on two fronts. The Schlieffen Plan only allowed for the Eastern Front to be garrisoned fairly lightly with a single army (the German Eighth Army) and they were very quickly badly outnumbered.

Initial Russian victories caused the German High Command to become duly concerned and they quickly brought in Paul von Hindenburg and Erich Ludendorff to sort out the mess. They promptly ordered a counter-attack to be launched in an effort to stabilise the front – which it did. They then put in place a bold attacking move, originally devised by Colonel Maximilian Hoffmann, which meant moving the bulk of their troops by train from the north to the south to face the Russian Second Army.

DID YOU KNOW?

Although exact figures are difficult to ascertain, German records suggest the Russians suffered 50,000 casualties (dead and wounded) and another 95,000 taken prisoner.

Part of the Russian master plan was that their First Army (commanded by General Rennenkampf) to the north would eventually spin round to the south-west to get closer to the Second Army (commanded by General Samsonov), providing a formidable joint force that would bulldoze its way into Germany. However, the First Army had had a rougher time of it than expected and had paused to reorganise after a tough scrap at Gumbinnen. They weren't coming to link up with the Second Army at all.

Communications between the two Russian armies were poor; they had over extended their communications lines and could no longer send encrypted messages. On 25 August, the Germans intercepted two messages which told them the distance between the two Russian armies and their relative marching plans; they now knew that if they attacked Samsonov in the south, Rennenkampf was too far away to offer any help.

DID YOU KNOW?

When the Russian Army took over the town of Allenstein, on 27 August, their first demand was for bread: 60,000 loaves to be delivered within ten hours.

I WAS THERE

I beg most humbly to report to Your Majesty that the ring round the larger part of the Russian Army was closed yesterday. The 13th. 15th and 18th Army Corps have been destroyed. We have already taken more than 60,000 prisoners, among them the Corps Commanders of the 13th and 15th Corps.

The guns are still in the forests and are now being brought in. The booty is immense though it cannot yet be assessed in detail. The Corps outside our ring, the 1st and 6th, have also suffered severely and are now retreating in hot haste through Mlawa and Myszaniec.

Paul von Hindenburg, in an official
report to Kaiser Wilhelm II, 31 August 1914[5]

DID YOU KNOW?

The Battle of Tannenberg did not take place at Tannenberg. It actually took place close to Allenstein, some 20 miles to the west. German High Command named the battle 'Tannenberg' after the event in an effort to blot out the defeat of the Teutonic Knights in the original Battle of Tannenberg in 1410 by a Polish-Lithuanian army.

On 27 August the Germans attacked Samsonov's north-eastern front with immediate success. The border town of Soldau was captured, destroying communication with Samsonov's central force. To capitalise on this success, a mass of German troops was sent from the north to encircle Samsonov's forces. Critically short of supplies, his exhausted troops in disarray and with no safe communication system, Samsonov had no choice but to give the order to retreat on 28 August. However, it was too late. By the 29th his forces were surrounded and cut off.

Out of an estimated 150,000 men at Samsonov's disposal, only 10,000 escaped. The Germans took 95,000 prisoners and 500 pieces of artillery. Samsonov committed suicide, while back in Germany Hindenburg and Ludendorff were lauded as heroes.

I WAS THERE

Samsonov said repeatedly that the disgrace of such a defeat was more than he could bear. 'The Emperor trusted me. How can I face him after such a disaster?' He went aside and his staff heard a shot. They searched for his body without success, but all are convinced that he shot himself. The Chief of Staff and other officers managed to reach Russian territory, having covered forty miles on foot.

Major General Sir Alfred Knox,
British liaison officer to the Imperial Russian Army ⁶

The news of the Russian defeat was a catastrophe for the Allies, so much so that the decision was made to keep the news away from the British public. But it wasn't a total disaster. In order to win this battle, Germany had been forced to transfer 85,000 men from the Western Front. This undoubtedly helped the cause of the French and the British at the Battle of the Marne and enabled them eventually to stop the German advance on Paris. They may not have known it at the time, but perhaps it was the Russians who had saved Paris?

THE FIRST BATTLE OF YPRES

TOWARDS THE END of 1914, both sides had resigned themselves to the fact that the war would not be a quick one. As the lines of trenches crept northwards in 'the race to the sea' both sides had their eye on a relatively small and peaceful town in Belgium: Ypres.

The British coveted the town because it served as a good transport hub for troops and supplies coming up from the French Channel ports. Germany saw it as a gateway to the rest of Belgium and control of the Belgian North Sea ports. Also, if they could control this area it would put severe pressure on British logistics.

Almost simultaneously both sides started to move troops into the area. Once again, the Allies were hopelessly outnumbered and, after assessing the situation, French General Ferdinand Foch decided the best thing to do was attack.

DID YOU KNOW?

Stories of the young German men singing as they marched to their death during their advance on 22 October became the stuff of legend – the Langemarck legend – on both sides of the line, and was used extensively by Nazi propagandists twenty years later.

32

I WAS THERE

The shrapnel is shrieking through the lane, I can hear the groans of our wounded. One man drops helplessly into our dug-out. He extends an arm battered beyond description. We bandage it. His groans are terrible. A shell bursts very near us. The shrapnel pieces fall through our roof. A piece strikes me on the shoulder. Luckily its force is spent.

Private Samuel Knight, 2nd Battalion, Welch Regiment[7]

He was hoping for a repeat performance of the First Battle of the Marne, where a surprise attack put the Germans on the defensive, despite their numerical advantage.

This time, however, he was to be disappointed.

Although there were initial isolated victories, the attacking Allied troops ran into wave after wave of German reinforcements, and despite repeated demands for more effort from over-eager commanding officers, the offensive ground to a halt by 20 October. It was now the Germans' turn to go on to the offensive.

They launched two simultaneous attacks: one directly against the Belgians at Dixmunde and the other straight at Ypres itself. The attack at Dixmunde was swift and powerful, and posed a real threat to the Channel ports. On 22 October, the German infantry, made up of volunteers and new draftees, some reportedly only 16 years of age, attacked the British at Bixschoote, singing as they advanced over open ground straight into British rifle and machine-gun fire. Not surprisingly, they were cut to pieces, with many battalions suffering up to 70 per cent casualties.

I WAS THERE

We pass through a perfect hail of shells up the Menin Road. Awful time! It's a wonder we're not blown to bits! We pass the infantry in reserve digging trenches as fast as they can. We get to the guns at last. They are all ready to be removed. Our gunners are very cool. The German infantry are not far from them. We can see them coming over the hill. There are not many of our infantry left.

Gunner C.B. Burrows, 104th Battery, 22nd Brigade, Royal Field Artillery

DID YOU KNOW?

The British Expeditionary Force suffered so many casualties during the First Battle of Ypres that it was effectively destroyed as a legitimate fighting force.

The Germans kept coming – an unstoppable wave of men and shells – but somehow, despite the British and Belgian forces being at the limits of physical and mental endurance, the line held long enough for the decision to be made to open the sluice gates that kept the North Sea out of Flanders.

Once these gates were opened the water levels in Flanders rose and provided a belt of marshland 20 miles long and 2 miles wide that protected the Allies from the German invaders. The attack around Dixmunde floundered and came to a stop. Ypres, on the other hand, had not flooded and was there for the taking. The Germans renewed their attacks on 31 October and immediately drove British cavalry from Messines Ridge. The British line, Ypres, and indeed the fate of the war, hung by a thread.

It seemed inevitable that Germany would take Ypres and Kaiser Wilhelm II arrived at the front in anticipation of leading his troops through the town on a victory march. On 11 November the elite Prussian guards launched a huge attack on the town, backed by the heaviest artillery bombardment witnessed so far on the Western Front. The situation was so bad for the British that cooks, orderlies and other support staff were forced to pick up rifles and bayonets to help repel the attack.

Casualties on both sides were horrific, with a total in excess of 250,000 men. Britain lost over 54,000 men killed, missing and wounded, but Ypres had been saved.

DID YOU KNOW?

German intelligence during the battle was poor. They consistently believed that the small numbers of enemy infantry were just outposts and had hugely overestimated the total strength of Allied forces.

NEUVE CHAPELLE

SO FAR THE war had not been fought on the back foot by the British. The previous eight months they had retreated, counter-attacked, marched, dug trenches by the mile and fought a defensive war. They were desperate to get on the offensive, and in early 1915 they got their wish.

The objective handed to the British First Army, led by Field Marshal Douglas Haig, was to take the village of Neuve Chapelle and then gain control of Aubers Ridge – a ridge of higher ground less than a mile to the east of the village that offered a commanding view of the surrounding area and would be an ideal launching pad for an advance towards German-held Lille.

DID YOU KNOW?

In the thirty-five minutes of artillery bombardment before the attack the British guns fired more shells than in the entire South African war of 1899–1902.

I WAS THERE

The opening bombardment was the most impressive that I think I heard throughout the war. It was quite brief and had only a limited amount of heavy artillery. It was nearly all field gun fire, but in the short period that it took place, the guns were fired at such a rapid rate that the noise was absolutely shattering. Where it was accurate against the German breastworks it had the most decisive effect, and our advancing infantry suffered only moderate losses.

Captain Philip Neame VC, 15th Field Company, Royal Engineers[9]

DID YOU KNOW?

The Battle of Neuve Chapelle was the first British-led offensive of the war, and saw them experiment with several innovations such as air reconnaissance, precision timetables for artillery and a dedicated light railway to take supplies to the front.

This was a new kind of war, a static war of attrition rather than fluid movements in the open that the British Army was more used to. However, Haig and his staff embraced the new challenges they faced; aerial reconnaissance provided intelligence of the size, position and depth of enemy defences, meticulous timetables were drawn up for the artillery – they even built a light railway to ensure supplies could be brought to the front in a timely manner.

At 7.30 a.m. on 10 March, the guns unleashed thirty-five minutes of hellfire directly on to the German front line. Haig wanted the bombardment to be much longer, but a shortage of shells forced his hand. At 8.05 a.m. the guns lifted and the infantry of the British First Army (including a large number of Indian troops) advanced along a 2-mile front.

I WAS THERE

We can only advance in short rushes, taking cover wherever possible, and it is impossible to keep the formation. We are about half a mile west of Neuve Chapelle, and the country is absolutely open, only slight depressions here and there.

Captain Wilfred Ewart, Scots Guards[10]

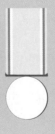

The guns then switched their attack to the rear of the German lines, in an effort to hamper the movement of reinforcements and supplies up to the front.

Just twenty-five minutes later British troops had captured the village of Neuve Chapelle.

However, such success was not evident along the whole of the front. There was a small part of the German line, situated nearest the ridge, which had not been bombarded at all. The wires were untouched, the machine-gun emplacements were not damaged and the enemy troops were still in their positions. The Indian soldiers who advanced on this sector in three successive waves stood no chance. Communication was so bad, though, that because no one returned back to their lines in this sector, HQ thought they had succeeded in their objective. The grisly fact was that they had all been killed or wounded.

Once the main breakthrough had been achieved, the successful attackers succumbed to a number of communication and supply issues that would blight both sides continually until the end of the war. Haig found it difficult, if not impossible, to keep in contact with his field commanders and as a consequence opportunities to advance were missed due to a lack of concrete orders.

DID YOU KNOW?

The battle had cost Britain and India 544 officers and 11,108 other ranks killed, missing or wounded. German losses are estimated at 12,000.

On the morning of 11 March, the British attacked once more. This time, however, the Germans were expecting them and the advancing infantry suffered terribly from machine-gun and artillery fire. Nonetheless, Haig ordered preparations to be made for a resumed offensive the next morning.

The Germans, however, had their own plan. Having soaked up two days of continual British attacks, now it was their turn. On the morning of 12 March, more than 10,000 German soldiers launched a counter-attack. Unfortunately for them it didn't succeed and, although they recovered some ground, the British held on to Neuve Chapelle. Just. This three-day battle had cost the Allies over 11,600 men killed, missing or wounded.

GALLIPOLI

WITH STALEMATE ON the Western Front and ever-increasing difficulties in maintaining reliable trade routes with Russia, the British were looking at other ways to kickstart their war effort. The Dardanelles ticked all the boxes: it connected the Black Sea to the Mediterranean, and if it could be captured, the route to Russia would be secured. Not only that, but victory in this area might tempt Greece and Bulgaria to join in the fight on the side of the Allies.

After an attempt to take the Dardanelle straits via a combined British and French naval attack failed, it was decided that the only way to gain ownership of the straits was to land ground troops on the peninsula. On 25 April 1915, 35,000 Anglo-French troops landed at Cape Helles, while 10 miles up the coast 17,000 members of the Australian and New Zealand Army Corps (Anzacs) headed towards Ari Burnu.

By 8 a.m. 8,000 Anzacs were ashore pushing themselves forward up steep terrain in the face of concentrated Turkish rifle fire. By nightfall they had only managed to get two-thirds of the way up the slope towards the plateau. With retreat impossible, the Anzacs had no choice but to dig in as best they could and prepare themselves to tough it out.

Meanwhile, further south, the Anglo-French landings, overseen by General Sir Ian Hamilton, enjoyed mixed fortunes. The three landings at 'Y', 'S', and 'X' beaches were practically unopposed and all forces got ashore with minimal fuss. However, at 'W' beach it was a different story.

Here the naval bombardment that had preceded the landings had failed to cut the underwater barbed wire or destroy much of the defence system around the beach. Nine hundred and fifty men of the Lancashire Fusiliers were sent towards that beach, but the Turks were waiting for them and by the time it was secured they had taken 543 casualties.

DID YOU KNOW?

On the morning of 25 April 1915, 950 men of the 1st Battalion, Lancashire Fusiliers, landed at 'W' beach. By the time the beach was secured they had suffered 543 casualties. Six Victoria Crosses were won on that beach that morning. 'Six VCs before breakfast' is a motto repeated with pride by the fighting men of Lancashire, and 'W' beach is now known as Lancashire Landing.

I WAS THERE

Dear Wang,

... I got through the landing without a scratch thanks to my natural instinct to seek cover on a flat beach, but sprained my ankle badly the second night falling in a trench in the dark. By Jove it was pretty hot that first Sunday morning. I can hardly write about it yet.

Poor old Porter was killed by a hand grenade I think climbing up the cliff on my right. I am awfully sick he got knocked over. Tom Maunsell and Tommy were shot getting out of the boat. Clark was shot through the head sitting in the boat. I tell you I looked pretty slippy about getting ashore. I jumped overboard in 5 feet of water. I don't think the men realised how hot the fire was they were laughing and joking to the last ... Well I think we fairly made a name for ourselves as we were first to establish a hold on the peninsular. I only got about five men ashore alive in my boat and not one of them could use their rifles owning to sand jamming the bolt.

Captain A.D. Talbot, 1st Battalion, Lancashire Fusiliers, from a letter of 2 May 2015[11]

At 'V' beach things were equally chaotic. An armoured troopship, *River Clyde*, was used to take the invaders close to the shore, but hidden Turkish defenders caused so many casualties in the first hour that a halt to the landings was ordered. They tried again that night, but by the time the beachhead had been secured, the assaulting troops had lost over half their men.

By nightfall on the 26th there were more than 30,000 Allied troops ashore; however, the Turkish troops were allowed to retire unmolested to a new line south of Krithia on 26 April. By the time the Allies were ready for an attack on the 28th, the Turks had reinforced their numbers to match those of the attackers. Stalemate ensued.

DID YOU KNOW?

The cost of this campaign was huge. Out of 480,000 Allied troops that took part, 252,000 ended up being casualties, with 48,000 dead. On the other side, it is estimated that the Turks took 250,000 casualties.

Over the coming months the Allies tried several times to advance but each attempted advance only added to the piles of dead bodies that littered the landscape. At Ari Burnu (soon to be renamed Anzac Cove) they didn't even attempt to break out. Such were the precarious positions that were held, coupled with a lack of men and supplies, that it was deemed best to stay put and wait for reinforcements.

Those reinforcements eventually appeared in August, along with a renewed offensive under the stewardship of Lieutenant General Sir Frederick Stopford. On 6 August, 20,000 men landed at Sulva Bay and encountered very little opposition; however, Stopford didn't give the order to push on inland until the evening. By this time the Turks had been alerted and quickly gathered five divisions to try to defend the area. By the time Stopford's men had reached the Tekke Tepe Ridge, the Turks were already there and greeted them with a bayonet charge. The opportunity for a quick victory had been lost.

DID YOU KNOW?

The Gallipoli campaign was the first time the Australian and New Zealand troops (Anzacs) went into action in the war.

I WAS THERE

It was pitch dark then all of a sudden the coast, a dim outline of the coast, loomed up. As we got closer, we were all beginning to get tensed up, nervous, wondering what was going to happen as everything was so quiet. Then a single shot rang out and a yellowish light flared up in the sky, and from then on the Turks let loose; machine gun and rifle fire at the boats. The pinnaces cast us off, the muffled oarsmen took up the row. As soon as the boats grounded it was every man for himself, it was out, do the best you could.

Private Walter Stagles, 3rd Australian Battalion, 1st Australian Division [12]

Despite continued attempts to advance, no extra ground was gained. Lord Kitchener visited the peninsula himself in November and promptly gave the order to evacuate.

Between 10 and 20 December, 105,000 men and 300 guns were successfully evacuated from Anzac Cove and Suvla Bay. Another 35,000 men were evacuated from Helles in late December and early January 1917.

LOOS

THE BATTLE OF Loos was set to be the biggest battle the British Army had fought in its history. It would be a joint Anglo-French affair with the advance taking place along a 20-mile front from Arras to La Bassée, with the objectives to wreak havoc on the intricate rail networks behind the German lines and cause as much damage to the German war effort as possible in the process.

Haig was not happy, though. He didn't like the look of the terrain he was being asked to advance over, plus he had a dire shortage of trained men as well as a distinct lack of guns and shells. However, he had to bow to political pressure and zero hour was set for 6.30 a.m. on 25 September 1915.

DID YOU KNOW?

The Battle of Loos saw the British use gas for the first time in warfare. In total, 5,100 cylinders of chlorine gas were released towards the German lines before the first attack. However, in places the wind blew the gas back into the British trenches, causing 2,632 gas casualties.

I WAS THERE

A little distance away from me three men hurried forward, and two of them carried a box of rifle ammunition. One of the bearers fell flat to the earth, his two mates halted for a moment, looked at the stricken boy, and seemed to puzzle at something. Then they caught hold of the box hangers and rushed forward. The man on the ground raised himself and looked after his mates, then sank down again to the wet ground. Another soldier came crawling towards us on his belly, looking for all the world like a gigantic lobster which had escaped from its basket. His lower lip was cut clean to the chin and hanging apart; blood welled through the muddy khaki trousers where they covered the hips.

Private Patrick Macgill, London Irish Rifles [13]

The preliminary bombardment for the attack started earlier on 21 September and continued until zero hour, when it moved to the German second line as per a meticulously prepared timetable. In total, 250,000 shells were fired in those four days in an effort to soften up the enemy defensive lines. Haig also had another weapon up his sleeve: gas. Haig gave the go ahead for its release at 5.50 a.m. on 25 September. Unfortunately, in many places along the front the wind was so light it took over forty-five minutes to get anywhere near the German lines, and in other places the gas actually blew back on to the attackers, causing 2,632 British casualties from their own gas attack.

The results of the advance were also decidedly mixed. In some areas the bombardment had failed to smash the enemy wire and positions. In these areas the attacking forces stood no chance and suffered terribly.

DID YOU KNOW?

Along most of the attacking front the Allies enjoyed significant numerical advantage, outnumbering German infantry in places as much as seven to one.

I WAS THERE

At first the gas drifted slowly towards the German lines (it was plainly visible owing to the rain) but at one or two bends of the trench the gas drifted into it. In these cases I had it turned off at once. At about 6.20am the wind changed and quantities of the gas came back over our own parapet, so I ordered all gas to be turned off and only smoke candles to be used.

Lieutenant A.B. White, 186 Company, Royal Engineers[19]

However, the town of Loos was captured, but poor communications with artillery support and the slow arrival of reserves meant that consolidation was impossible. The attack eventually came to a halt with troops pinned down by severe machine-gun fire on the crest of Hill 70.

By nightfall on the 27th the attacking troops were practically spent, with Hill 70 and other strategic positions still in German hands. Once again the advance had broken into the enemy positions but had failed to go beyond.

Sporadic fighting continued until 13 October, but the situation did not change. More than 61,000 casualties were sustained in the Battle of Loos. Kitchener's New Army units rushed into the line after being in France a matter of days and suffered terribly – but they had proven they had what it takes to be a soldier on the Western Front.

DID YOU KNOW?

The Battle of Loos was the first time the men from Kitchener's New Armies went into battle on the Western Front.

JUTLAND

FOR YEARS GERMANY had been busy building up her naval fleet to make it a match for the Royal Navy, and by the outbreak of war both countries possessed significant naval power. The Royal Navy were keen to show the world that they still ruled the waves, whereas the Kaiser was obsessed with destroying Britain's Grand Fleet.

By 1916, both fleets were straining at the leash and ready to go. The absence of aircraft at sea meant that figuring out the whereabouts of the enemy was down to decoding enemy messages, vigilant lookouts and a bit of guesswork. On 31 May 1916 neither side really knew where the other was until scouting cruisers from both sides made contact as they both investigated a stationary Danish merchant ship. All of a sudden the naval war was on.

DID YOU KNOW?

The Royal Navy lost more men and ships (6,097 killed, 14 ships lost) than the German fleet (2,551 killed, 11 ships lost).

DID YOU KNOW?

After hearing news of the battle Kaiser Wilhelm II boasted that 'the spell of Trafalgar is broken'.[15]

It was the German High Seas Fleet that drew first blood. Admiral Beatty, commanding the British battlecruisers, engaged with the enemy and chased them to the south; both sets of battlecruisers exchanged broadsides as they travelled along parallel courses. The British suffered badly, losing HMS *Indefatigable* and HMS *Queen Mary*. In addition, HMS *Lion*, HMS *Tiger* and HMS *Princess Royal* were badly damaged.

On top of this, Beatty soon learned that he was heading straight towards the entire German fleet. He immediately ordered his ships to turn about and head north towards Admiral Jellicoe and the remainder of the British Grand Fleet. He hoped the Germans would give chase so he could lead them into a trap. The Germans did indeed follow, and they got a nasty surprise when they fell under a huge bombardment from Jellicoe's battle fleet, which they thought had been too far north to be of any consequence.

I WAS THERE

A few more rounds were fired when I took another look through my telescope and there was quite a fair distance between the second ship and what I believed was the fourth ship, due I think to [the] third ship going under. Flames were belching from what I took to be the fourth ship of the line, then came the big explosion which shook us a bit, and on looking at the pressure gauge I saw the pressure had failed. Immediately after that came, what I term, the big smash, and I was dangling in the air on a bowline, which saved me from being thrown down on the floor of the turret.

Petty Officer Ernest Francis, HMS Queen Mary[16]

Admiral Scheer soon found himself surrounded to the north and north-west. The only option was to turn east. The Grand Fleet threw everything they had at Scheer, who ordered an about turn to every ship in his command. Executed perfectly, within a few minutes the German High Seas Fleet slipped into the murk and out of sight. The British were sure they had sunk a number of ships, but in reality only one was lost. On the other hand, the British had lost HMS *Warrior* and HMS *Invincible*, and HMS *Warspite* was severely damaged.

As the Germans fled, Jellicoe refused to follow directly, fearful of a minefield or submarine trap. Instead he turned south-east, then south in an effort to cut Scheer off indirectly. Then, inexplicably, Scheer turned his fleet to the north, and basically steamed straight back into the heart of the Grand Fleet. Within twenty minutes, one German destroyer was sunk and many damaged before the German fleet were able to about turn and retreat.

DID YOU KNOW?
The Battle of Jutland was the largest naval battle of the war.

I WAS THERE

Two or three hits shake the ship further aft. One of these bursts in the lower deck, between C and D turrets, causing serious casualties in the after action dressing station, among the wounded, surgeons and sick-bay attendants. At the same time it destroys part of the power leads to D turret ... This shell also tears up the main armoured deck, the only case of this happening, but does no damage to the powder magazines just underneath it.

Commander Paschen, SMS Lützow [17]

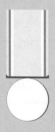

This time Jellico went on the chase, heading south-west in an effort to intercept, which he did just before sunset. The guns flashed in the gathering gloom and more German ships were destroyed and damaged. At 8.30 p.m. Scheer sent six of his ships forward to occupy the British guns while he gathered the rest of his fleet and fled to the west.

The Battle of Jutland, the largest and the last great naval encounter, was over. After the battle the Germans celebrated it as a great victory, and indeed they did lose less ships than the British. Conversely, in Britain the mood was one of disappointment. The public had expected a crushing victory – another Trafalgar. However, the British Fleet was straight back in training and was ready to fight again by June, whereas the German High Fleet was crippled for months and was never risked again in a North Sea battle.

VERDUN

BY 1916 IT was clear that if Germany was to succeed on the Western Front it needed a change in tactics. Even though a major breakthrough into Paris was going to be unlikely, France could still be defeated through attrition. What Germany needed to instigate was a huge all-out fight that would consume all of the French resources and manpower until there was nothing left. For this plan to work they would need a target that the French would defend until the last man, regardless of losses. That place was Verdun: a fortress city with a special place in French hearts, emotionally more than strategically, and Eric von Falkenhayn, the German Chief of Staff, knew the French would defend it until the last man if necessary.

Verdun was a perfect choice for the attack: the city was only lightly defended as many of the big fortress guns had been removed for use elsewhere along the front, and logistics and communications greatly favoured the attackers.

DID YOU KNOW?

In the opening bombardment, German guns fired over 1 million shells on to Verdun in just nine hours.

I WAS THERE

*Over the roads leading towards Verdun,
artillery and ammunition were brought up in
such quantities as the history of war has never
seen on such a small space. The country was
covered with guns ... Long rows of guns as in
old battle pictures, set up in open fields with
gunners standing about them, and on the
hill-tops observation posts with their great
telescopes uncovered.*

German eyewitness, Verdun, 1916[11]

DID YOU KNOW?

The French estimate losses at around 550,000 men, with the German losses estimated at over 450,000. About half of all casualties were killed.

On 21 February 1916 an artillery bombardment, the likes of which had never been witnessed before, started. In just nine hours, 1,220 German guns fired over 1 million shells on to Verdun. At 4 p.m. that day, the guns lifted and the assaulting infantry advanced. Those French soldiers who had somehow survived the bombardment fought heroically and defended to the death, inch by inch, but gradually the overwhelming attacking force took its toll and the Germans advanced on, albeit slowly. In some places advances of only one-third of a mile or so had been achieved, instead of the 7 or 8 miles that were planned.

Eventually, on 24 February, they broke through the French first line. The second line fell soon afterwards, and the third line was not yet built. The Germans were 5 miles from Verdun, and not much stood in their way.

On the 26th, in an effort to halt the inevitable, General Pétain was put in charge of the French Army at Verdun. Pétain immediately reorganised the line and orchestrated a more robust artillery response. He also made sure the supply routes to the front were kept open at all times; this made a huge difference as new men, weapons and equipment finally arrived at the front. By the 28th the German offensive had started to bog down, and the French were beginning to retaliate with artillery fire of their own.

The Germans tried again with several huge attacks and succeeded in capturing the town of Fleury on 23 June. At this time General Robert Nivelle, recently promoted to the command of the French Second Army, issued an Order of the Day which ended with the infamous rallying cry: *Ils ne passeront pas!* (They shall not pass!)

Fighting continued throughout the summer and autumn, but the tables were slowly turning. Indeed, it was the French that started to advance with a series of successful counter-attacks throughout October and November – and Fleury was back in French hands by 24 October. By mid-December the Germans had been pushed back far enough to render Verdun safe.

DID YOU KNOW?

At least 70 per cent of all casualties from the Battle of Verdun were due to artillery fire.

I WAS THERE

The situation is not brilliant; nevertheless I am holding at Samogneux ... all the horses have been killed, bicycles smashed, runners wounded or scattered along all the routes. I shall be doing the impossible if I keep you informed of events.

Lieutenant Colonel Bernard, Commanding Officer 351st Regiment, in a message to Divisional HQ on 23 February 1916[13]

THE SOMME

THE SOMME OFFENSIVE was the main Allied attack along the Western Front in 1916. It was originally planned to be a French attack with British support, with the main objective of smashing the German Army and depleting their resources of manpower and supplies. As such, it was the French who chose the Somme region as the location of the advance; Haig didn't like this area of ground but the politics of the situation forced his hand and the Somme offensive was agreed and scheduled for August 1916.

However, the situation at Verdun forced a change in these carefully laid plans. It was clear that France would not be in any fit state to lead a major offensive; in fact, it was touch and go as to whether they would survive as a fighting unit. They needed help from Britain to divert German manpower and resources away from Verdun, and they needed it fast.

DID YOU KNOW?

Over a million men became casualties during this bitter struggle, with Britain and her empire suffering to the tune of 419,654 men wounded and killed.

I WAS THERE

I don't exaggerate when I say nearly 100,000 shells dropped that day in an area of about 800 square yards.

Reverend A. Caseby, Royal Army Chaplain Division, diary entry for 31 August 1916, from Trones Wood, just outside Guillemont [20]

DID YOU KNOW?

On the first day of the battle, 1 July 1916, the British Army suffered 57,740 casualties, including 19,240 killed.

So the Somme offensive would now be a large-scale British diversionary attack aimed at moving as many German troops away from Verdun as possible to relieve the pressure on the French Army. Planning was passed over to Haig and they had little time to lose; instead of August, the offensive would now take place on 1 July.

Known by the soldiers as the 'Big Push', this was the largest offensive that the British Army had ever planned in its history. Eight days before zero hour the preliminary bombardment started to smash the German positions and those guns did not stop until it was time for the infantry, some 750,000 men (of which a large percentage was made up from Kitchener's new Pals battalions), to advance. The guns were supposed to destroy German defences, cut their wire and shatter the resolve and morale of the enemy soldiers; the advancing Allied soldiers would need to do nothing more than take prisoners and consolidate their positions.

I WAS THERE

We were under an extraordinary heavy fire, and suffered accordingly, but the troops holding the sectors of trench under attack stood along the fire-steps of the parapet and awaited the enemy with rifles and machine guns. The waves of assaulting troops came under the concerted fire of all our weapons, and only isolated parties got as far as our wire.

Albrecht Stosch, 66th Infantry Regiment[21]

I WAS THERE

The barbed wire that was supposed to have been demolished had only been cut in places. Just a gap here, a gap there, and everyone made for the gaps in order to get through. There were supposed to be no Germans at all in the front line – but they were down in the ground in their concrete shelters. They just fired at the breeches in the wire and mowed us down. It seemed to me, eventually, that I was the only man left ... All I could see were men lying dead, men screaming, men on the barbed wire with their bowels hanging down, shrieking, and I thought, 'What can I do?'

Corporal Don Murray, 8th Battalion, King's Own Yorkshire Light Infantry[22]

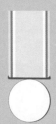

Unfortunately, a mixture of poor-quality ammunition and world-class underground German bunkers resulted in the general failure of the bombardment. Wire was not cut, morale had not been broken, defences were still intact and, when the infantry attacked the German positions at 7.30 a.m. on 1 July, the German machine-gunners and artillery were ready and waiting.

What happened in the next few hours stands to this day as the darkest moment in the British Army's illustrious history. The advancing troops suffered over 58,000 casualties, a third of which were killed. Apart from the odd isolated success, the large bulk of the British infantry was either cut down in no-man's-land or forced back to their own lines. Ironically, it was the French that made the best progress towards the south of the front.

DID YOU KNOW?

On 31 August 1916, Harry Butters, a young US citizen serving with the British Royal Field Artillery, was killed, becoming the first American casualty of the First World War.

Despite everything, Haig persisted with the offensive in the following days. Advances were made, but these were limited and mostly repulsed. On 11 July, the first line of German trenches was secured. On that day German troops were transferred from Verdun to contribute to the German defence, doubling the number of men available. The fighting continued until the November snow forced the end of the battle. Both sides had enjoyed minor successes in isolated battles but no major breakthrough was gained. Even the tank, which made its operational debut during the Battle of Flers-Courcelette on 15 September, failed to make a great impact due to reliability issues and a lack of tactical expertise.

At the end of it all, the Allied forces had gained a slither of tortured landscape 8 miles across at the deepest point, but that really wasn't the issue. The offensive did achieve its desired effect: to inflict huge casualties on the Germans and relieve the pressure on the French at Verdun. With this in mind, Haig could be excused for saying 'job done'.

THE BRUSILOV OFFENSIVE

WHILE THE WESTERN Front was flexing under the weight of the fighting at Verdun, the Russians were weighing up their options in the east. On 15 May 1916, the Austrians launched a significant attack on the Trentino region and threatened to overwhelm the Italian Army; the Russians were asked to intervene. Despite general reluctance, one Russian officer, Aleksei Brusilov, thought he could knock Austria out of the Italian front with only minimal equipment and reinforcements.

Brusilov put together a different kind of offensive than had been seen previously, using speed and surprise across a broad front to confuse the enemy and make it more difficult to launch effective counter-attacks.

Preparation was meticulous and methodical as Brusilov's men were going to attack a well-defended line made up of deep trenches, mines, electric fences and thick barbed wire.

DID YOU KNOW?

With an estimated total casualty list of over 2.5 million men, the Brusilov Offensive was one of the most deadly battles in world history.

I WAS THERE

[Army Group] Benigni is not capable of resistance. There is at present absolutely no possibility of holding against an enemy attack. The decision to attempt it would lead to the total destruction [of Army Group Benigni].

Cavalry General Karl von Pfanzer-Baltin VI, Commander of Austrian Seventh Army, in a note of 11 June 1916[23]

I WAS THERE

It was a pitiful parade. Endless columns of horse-drawn vehicles in one row after another with artillery placed in between ... The troops came from all sides, tired and harassed.

Austrian soldier describing the retreat of the Austrian Army between 10 and 11 June 1916[24]

Detailed plans of the enemy lines were drawn up, guns were to be concealed, and troops and supplies were hidden in underground bunkers. If any overt preparations were needed, they were carried out up and down the entire line so as to give no clue as to the location of any attack. Reserves were to be brought right up to the front, so they could take advantage of any breakthrough, and artillery officers would also be directing fire right from the front line.

Brusilov's men dug advance trenches less than 330ft from the Austro-Hungarian front lines and waited for zero hour.

When the guns opened up on the morning of 4 June, in the northern sector of the line, it was short, sharp and very accurate. Much of the first defensive line of the Austrians was smashed to pieces and the attacking Russian infantry encountered little trouble as they set about consolidating their gains. As they drove deeper into enemy territory, shock troops went out in front, seeking out the weak points of the line, cutting communication lines and generally causing havoc, allowing reserves to follow in numbers. The Austrians in the north were being routed and the alarm was quickly sounded to HQ – reinforcements were needed. Fast.

I WAS THERE

Every man in the army must be aware that he is fighting here to decide the campaign, and to decide the fate of the Fatherland.

Austro-Hungarian High Command, proclamation to troops, June 1916[25]

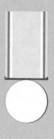

In the south, another crisis was brewing for the Austrians. The Russians had also attacked on the Romanian border and were causing all kinds of trouble down there. The Austrian Army was on the retreat – but where to send the reserves? Reserves could not be placed effectively and as a result the entire army was being pushed backwards. It was chaos.

The Russians pushed forward with wild enthusiasm. They had quickly advanced over 60 miles, taking 350,000 prisoners en route. In emergency meetings the German Chief of Staff, von Falkenhayn, persuaded the Austrians to retreat and fall back to a more stable line close to good railway links. Von Falkenhayn was forced to move four German divisions out of Verdun to bolster the Austrians. This weakening of the Verdun army allowed a successful French counter-attack on 23 June, just one day before the opening salvos of the British preliminary bombardment on the Somme.

DID YOU KNOW?

Brusilov was dubbed 'The Iron General', although he was respected and beloved by his men. He demanded absolute preparedness for battle and expected his orders to be obeyed to the letter, down to the most minute detail.

DID YOU KNOW?

In the space of three months the Russians pushed the front lines westward as much as 30 miles in the central areas of the front and up to 75 miles in the south.

Meanwhile, the Russian advance was slowing down. The troops were exhausted and had stretched supply lines to breaking point. They had run out of ammunition and water, and had little or no communications with each other. As a result, Brusilov's forces advanced on two lines within their sector that went in the opposite direction to each other, thus diminishing their effectiveness. The spectacular gains of the first weeks had dried up and by mid-August the attack had pretty much spluttered to a halt.

With over a million casualties on either side, this was one of the deadliest battles of the war. However, it was deemed a success; the German Army had been forced to move significant men and resources away from Verdun and the Austrian-Hungarian Army was practically destroyed: they would not be able to launch another meaningful attack again.

THE BATTLE OF MESSINES RIDGE & THIRD YPRES

MESSINES RIDGE DOMINATED the flat landscape to the south of Ypres and as such held huge strategic importance for the armies battling it out in this part of Belgium. It had been in German hands since 1914, but the British wanted it back. Haig agreed with his commanders that it would be easier to blow the ridge to pieces rather than try a full frontal assault up the sides. The tunnelling commenced in early 1916 and by early June 1917 there were 5 miles of tunnels containing nineteen separate mines ready to blow Messines Ridge apart.

At 3.10 a.m. on 7 June 1917, the mines were detonated. Synchronised with deadly effect, every available gun the Allies had in the area also started to fire upon the ridge, giving the advancing Allied infantry a protective curtain of fire. Isolated German strongpoints put up some resistance but these were eventually knocked out. By 5 p.m. all objectives had been captured and by 14 June the entire Messines Salient was in Allied hands.

DID YOU KNOW?

At the height of the tunnelling activity under Messines Ridge there were about 20,000 British, Canadian, Australian and New Zealand tunnellers digging holes in the ridge, with about as many Germans tunnelling towards them.

I WAS THERE

About a hundred yards in front of us was a bank which extended for hundreds of yards across the ground behind which the Australians were. Our chaps charged through them to take a position in front, and Captain Mann, our adjutant, who was following close behind, fell with a bullet through his head.

Private Frank Richards DCM MM, 2nd Royal Welch Fusiliers[26]

With the success at Messines, Haig was convinced that the German Army was there for the taking and one last push in the Ypres Salient would push the enemy even farther back and allow Britain to gain control of the north Belgian coastal ports – home to German U-boats that were inflicting heavy losses on the Royal Navy.

After a giant ten-day preliminary bombardment over 260,000 British and French troops under the command of British General Gough advanced from Ypres at 3.50 a.m. on 31 July towards the village of Passchendaele – their ultimate objective, some 4½ miles distant. Initial progress was good; Pilckem Ridge was captured and the advance carried on in good time. At about 2 p.m., the Germans launched a massive counter-attack that pushed the Allies back to the ridge. It was at around this time the rain came.

DID YOU KNOW?

When the mines were detonated under Messines Ridge the eruption was so loud it was clearly heard in London and other parts of southern England.

I WAS THERE

Suddenly the fire from the pill box eased, and a shout from the next shell hole just reached my ears. I turned and saw a sergeant looking in my direction. 'Fire at that trench,' came faintly through the uproar. I turned and nodded, and saw with a feeling of sickness the tin hat jump violently off the man's head, and the immediate fading of life as a bullet crashed through the brain.

Private Arthur Lambert, Honourable Artillery Company[27]

I WAS THERE

Here was a stretcher-party staggering along the wet duckboards with a horrid burden from which the blood leaked and splattered; they moved with uncertain footings, their shoulders sagging with the load, and as they reached our line of dug-outs there came the scream of a shell, a huge flash, a rending explosion, and the stretcher party vanished.

Signaller Aubrey Wade, Royal Field Artillery[28]

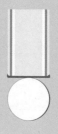

DID YOU KNOW?

Between 21 and 31 July more than 3,000 Allied guns fired over 4 million shells on to the German defensive lines prior to the initial advance towards the village of Passchendaele.

Heavy rain quickly turned the Flanders lowlands into a mud-churned swamp and effectively halted any chance of further advancement. A month of fighting in atrocious conditions followed. It became virtually impossible to move men, animals, equipment, supplies and artillery, but Gough urged his men on and on, making him very unpopular. Eventually Haig transferred control of the offensive to General Plumer on 25 August, who implemented his 'Bite and Hold' formula to good effect once the rain had subsided, taking the Gheluvelt Plateau, Polygon Wood and Broodseinde in quick succession. The rain, however, returned with a vengeance and caused chaos for the Allies preparing for the next advance on Passchendaele Ridge and the village beyond, scheduled for dawn on 9 October. Once more it was almost impossible to rearrange the artillery and get them in the correct positions to support the coming attack.

Many were stuck in their original positions, which meant that their upcoming targets were either at the extreme limits of their range or out of range completely. When the attacking infantry went over the top that morning, with little or no artillery support, it was no surprise that it ended in abject failure with enormous casualties. Three days later the attack was repeated, with a sadly inevitable result.

Despite requests to call off the advance, Haig and Plumer went ahead with one more attempt to secure Passchendaele ridge and take the village, this time using Canadian troops. The weather improved and by the time the Canadians started their assault on 26 October they could enjoy much more effective artillery support. The terrain was still awful and the men had to advance through some of the worst conditions of the war, but despite this they inched up the ridge towards the village, eliminating strongpoints one by one. By nightfall on 30 October they were just 500 yards from Passchendaele village, which finally fell on 10 November.

After the battle, the renowned war correspondent Sir Philip Gibbs KBE noted the following:

The enemy may brush aside our capture of Passchendaele as the taking of a mud patch, but to resist it he has at one time or another put nearly a hundred divisions into the arena of blood, and the defence has cost him a vast sum of loss in dead and wounded. I saw his dead in Inverness Copse and Glencorse Wood, and over all this ground where the young manhood of Germany lies black and in corruption.

CAMBRAI

AFTER THE MESS of the Flanders offensive around Ypres and Passchendaele, Haig was keen to end 1917 on a high. He turned to the Tank Corps and ordered them to plan a direct attack on the much-fabled German defensive area known as the Hindenburg Line, with the German-held town of Cambrai at its heart. Zero hour was to be dawn on 20 November 1917.

At 6.20 a.m. that morning the massed artillery barked into life along a relatively short front. There was no prolonged artillery bombardment this time: surprise was of the essence, as was keeping the ground as flat and unbroken by shell fire as possible to allow good progress of the tanks.

Over 300 tanks drove forward that morning, backed by the massed ranks of the infantry. It was the first time in the history of warfare that such numbers of tanks had been used as the primary weapon in an offensive operation.

DID YOU KNOW?

For this battle, the Royal Artillery used a system of pre-registering the accuracy of their guns before zero hour for the first time. This enabled them to carry out counter-battery work and lay down a barrage on the enemy front lines simultaneously.

I WAS THERE

The first thing I noticed as I raised the nose of my tank to cross over the trench was several grey-clad bodies lying right in my path, and just as the bus gave her downward lurch one of them turned and looked up in a most despairing effort to avoid the monster. I'm afraid there were many that day that suffered a similar fate.

Driver A.W. Bacon, 5th Battalion, Tank Corps[23]

I WAS THERE

My section crossed the front line at a quarter past seven, and the infantry, with whom we were to co-operate, followed the two main-body tanks from there at a distance of about seventy yards. Utterly bewildered, the enemy was surrendering in panic in all directions.

Captain D.E. Hickey, Tank Corps[30]

They were effective too, crushing barbed wire and other defences with little effort. By the end of the day the much-vaunted Hindenburg Line had been broken, especially on the north of the front where advances of several miles were recorded.

This initial breakthrough was, by Western Front standards at least, a huge success and was just what Haig needed after the nightmare of Passchendaele. However, the British had lost 179 tanks during this first day, and the momentum of attack was quickly lost.

The following day the Germans pushed a new division, fresh from the Eastern Front, into the weakest parts of their line and succeeded in stemming the British tide. Any thoughts of a breakthrough were quashed. Indeed, it was now time for the Germans to counter-attack, and with pockets of fresh men armed with mobile weapons such as light machine guns, grenades and light mortars, the momentum quickly shifted in their favour. Within a week the German Army had recaptured the ground that was originally lost.

DID YOU KNOW?
After the initial successes church bells were rang across Britain for the first time since 1914.

KAISERSCHLACHT

AFTER THE BITTER battles of 1917, the German High Command was of the opinion that the British were exhausted and ready to be defeated once and for all. In their view, if Britain was knocked out of the war, the French would have no choice but to negotiate for peace. However, with American presence becoming stronger by the month, if Germany had any hopes of making this situation a reality they had to go on the offensive. And fast. Ludendorff came up with a master plan, code-named *Kaiserschlacht* (King's Battle), which he hoped would smash the British Army into surrender.

There were to be four separate attacks (code-named Michael, Georgette, Blücher-Yorck and Gneisenau). Michael would be the main attack and was scheduled for 21 March 1918.

DID YOU KNOW?

The initial advance was so spectacular that the Kaiser was certain of total victory. He awarded Hindenburg the Iron Cross with Golden Rays, last awarded to Prince Blücher after the Battle of Waterloo.

I WAS THERE

It is absolute Hell here. Cold-blooded murder and mass slaughter. The Germans in their mass formation get it from our Lewis and machine-guns while they give it to us unmercifully with their artillery. The fatigue is awful and the strain of holding on tremendous, and God knows how long it will go on.

Private Arthur Wrench, 1/4 Battalion, Seaforth Highlanders in a diary entry for 22 March 1918[31]

I WAS THERE

We knew what the orders were; they must not break through. If retirement, and it will be necessary, retire but don't let them break through. That was all our orders and that's what we did, that's what we did from 21st March; nine days and ten nights of scrapping and retiring ...

Sergeant Ernest Bryan, 17th Battalion, King's Liverpool Regiment[32]

DID YOU KNOW?

For the opening offensive of Operation Michael, on 21 March 1918, the Germans had seventy-four infantry divisions (roughly 910,000 men) lined up to go 'over the top'.

The initial advance was a success with elite storm troopers penetrating deep into Allied territory, knocking out strongpoints that allowed the massed infantry to follow quickly to consolidate the gains. The British had no choice but to execute a fighting retreat. In a distinct case of déjà vu from 1914, the Germans gave chase but quickly became exhausted as they over-extended their supply lines. The advance slowed down considerably and gave the Allies a chance to rush fresh troops in to stem the tide. In the first German push they had advanced 40 miles – a remarkable feat – but they had failed to break the British lines.

Another large attack, Georgette, commenced on 9 April, with an attack zone of about 25 miles running from 6 miles east of Ypres to 6 miles east of Bethune, centring on the River Lys. The main force of this attack centred in the Neuve Chapelle area, normally a quiet sector and lightly held. At the time of the attack the 2nd Portuguese Division were in residence.

DID YOU KNOW?

Although exact numbers are impossible to ascertain, it is estimated that the four German offensives of spring 1918 resulted in over 1.5 million total casualties.

When the attack came they didn't stand a chance and were quickly overrun. Up and down the front the Germans were rampant and heading quickly towards the coast. On 14 April, French General Ferdinand Foch became General-in-Chief of all Allied armies, giving him the power to move French, British and other Allied resources around as he saw fit. He quickly reorganised the defensive line and pushed fresh French troops into the fight in an effort to stop the advance. Numerous localised battles continued, but once again the Germans had outpaced their supply lines and were slowing down. By the end of April it was clear that Operation Georgette was not going to meet its objectives.

The focus of the attack now switched further south, around the River Aisne, in phase three (Blücher-Yorck) of Kaiserschlacht. Once more initial gains were impressive: first-day advances were up to 10 miles in places and by 3 June the German Army was only 55 miles from Paris, but an inability to keep supply chains of rations and ammunition intact, along with general fatigue and a lack of reinforcements meant that, once more, the German attack just fizzled out, this time just short of Amiens.

With one final throw of the dice, Ludendorff launched his next offensive – Gneisenau – aimed at breaking through the French lines around the River Oise, in an effort to flatten out the salient created by the Blücher-Yorck attack. However, the French knew they were coming and organised themselves accordingly, retreating back from their front lines to ready themselves for a counter-attack. The attackers struck forwards once more, and by 10 June they were just 45 miles from France, but the next day a huge Franco-American counter-attack, with the aid of full air support and over 150 tanks, succeeded in stopping the Germans in their tracks.

Ludendorff called off the attack on 12 June after just four days.

THE BATTLE
OF AMIENS

AFTER SUCCESSFULLY HALTING the German offensives of 1918, the Allied High Command met and decided what to do next. The general consensus was that the war was likely to continue into 1919, but General Foch was keen on a number of counter-attacks in 1918 specifically to flatten out the troublesome salients at St Mihiel, Château-Thierry and Amiens. The British were asked to help out at Amiens, a task handed to General Rawlinson and his Fourth Army.

By the early hours of 8 August, thousands of British, Canadian and Australian troops, backed up by around 500 tanks, were huddled in front-line trenches waiting to start the advance. There would be no preliminary bombardment for this advance as Rawlinson wanted to use the element of surprise on the enemy.

And surprise them he did. The tanks and the infantry advanced together at 4.20 a.m. behind a protective curtain of fire from the Allied artillery. The German guns were eerily quiet; the counter-battery work being carried out by the Royal Artillery was obviously working well.

DID YOU KNOW?

By 11 August there were only six operational tanks left from a starting force of over 500.

I WAS THERE

The tanks crept forward, I followed the one in front, and just as we neared the deploying spot a blinding flash knocked me backwards, causing me to cut my head on the steel bolts behind me, and blinding me temporarily ...Another terrific crash shook the whole machine, and as I peered forward I noticed smoke rising from the tank in front and saw its left trackband rearing into the air like a cobra preparing to strike.

The officer of that bus dashed round to me and said: 'Swing out and pass us. My driver's killed. Got a direct hit.' Poor Sergeant Sutton.

Driver A.W. Bacon, 5th Battalion, Tank Corps[33]

DID YOU KNOW?

On the first day of the battle Germany suffered 30,000 casualties, along with another 20,000 taken prisoner. These statistics led Ludendorff to remark that the first day of the Battle of Amiens was 'the black day of the German Army'.

By early afternoon, the Canadian and Australians in the centre of the attack had advanced about 7 miles and the Germans were surrendering in their thousands. It wasn't quite as easy to the north (British) and to the south (French) of the attacking front. Here some of the German guns had escaped the attention of the Royal Artillery and provided stiff resistance to the attackers. The British attack managed to advance 2 miles but failed to take the high ground around Chipilly.

The fighting continued into the next day, but without the same momentum. The advance stretched communication and supply systems to their limit; they had advanced too fast for the artillery to keep up with the new-found mobility. The Germans had also poured in fresh reserves and were beginning to put up a much greater fight. The offensive slowly ground to a halt. By 11 August, with a handful of working tanks left, Rawlinson proposed that the focus of the attack be switched to the neighbouring Third Army.

I WAS THERE

In the summer of 1918 came the breakthrough. We had left the trenches behind, those mud sodden trenches that we hated for so many years. We were out in the open country. We almost felt victory in the air.

Sergeant Major Richard Tobin, Hood Battalion, Royal Naval Division[34]

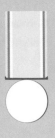

DID YOU KNOW?

On 11 August Ludendorff met with the Kaiser and told him bluntly that the war was lost. He also offered his resignation but the Kaiser refused to accept it.

The Battle of Amiens was over, but the Third Army took up the baton with a fresh attack across the old Somme battlefield of 1916. Fighting across open country, the town of Bapaume was eventually captured by New Zealand infantry on 29 August; two days later the Australians had captured Peronne and finally the Canadians broke through the German lines south-east of Arras, causing the enemy to abandon the Somme region and retreat all the way back to the Hindenburg Line.

The Battle of Amiens and the subsequent fighting on the Somme constituted the last great battle of the war. It was the battle that finally broke the hearts and minds of the German Army, after which they abandoned any realistic hope of ultimate victory.

NOTES

1   Bloem, Walter, *Vormarsch* (Nabu Press, 2010).

2   Hammerton, John (ed.), *The Great War ... I Was There!* (The Amalgamated Press Ltd, 1939), p. 44.

3   Ibid., p. 149.

4   IWM Sound Archive, cat. no. 212.

5   Horne, Charles F. (ed.), *Records of the Great War*, Vol. II (National Alumni, 1923).

6   Knox, Sir A., *With the Russian Army: 1914–1917* (Hutchinson, 1921).

7   Beckett, Ian F.W., *Ypres: The First Battle 1914* (Pearson Longman, 2006).

8   Macdonald, Lyn, *1914: The Days of Hope* (Penguin, 1989).

9   IWM Sound Archive, cat. no. 48.

10 Hammerton, op. cit., p. 312.

11 Reproduced with kind permission of the copyright holder, Captain (retd) Joe Eastwood BEM CQSW (www.lancs-fusiliers. co.uk).

12 IWM Sound Archive, cat. no. 4240.

13 Hammerton, op. cit., p. 468.

14 Macdonald, Lyn, *1915* (Penguin, 1997).

15 The National Archives, document ref. MFQ 1/366.

16 Moynihan, Michael (ed.), *People at War 1914–1918* (David & Charles, 1973).

17 Hammerton, op. cit., p. 648.

18 Horne, Charles F. & Austin, Warren F. (eds),
    Great Events of the Great War (National
    Alumni, 1920).
19 Horne, Alistair, *The Price of Glory* (Penguin,
    1986).
20 IWM, cat. no. OMD 3440.
21 von Stosh, Albrecht, *Somme Nord, Die
    Brennpunkte der Schlacht im Juli 1916*
    (I.O.G. Stalling, 1927).
22 IWM Sound Archive, cat. no. 25548.
23 Dowling, T.C., *The Brusilov Offensive*
    (Indiana University Press, 2008).
24 Ibid.
25 Ibid.
26 Hammerton, op. cit., p. 1291.
27 Ibid., p. 1320.
28 Ibid., p. 1361.
29 Ibid., p. 1443.
30 Ibid., p. 1452.
31 Brown, Malcolm, *The Imperial War
    Museum Book of 1918* (Sidgwick & Jackson,
    1998).
32 IWM Sound Archive, cat. no. 4042.
33 Hammerton, op. cit., p. 1753.
34 IWM Sound Archive, cat. no. 4243.

BIBLIOGRAPHY

Addington, Scott, *The First World War Fact Book* (Independently published, 2013)

Addington, Scott, *World War One: A Layman's Guide* (Independently published, 2012)

Barton, Peter & Banning, Jeremy, *The Battlefields of the First World War* (Constable, 2013)

Beckett, Ian F.W., Ypres: *The First Battle 1914* (Pearson Longman, 2006)

Dowling, Timothy C., *The Brusilov Offensive* (Indiana University Press, 2008)

Doyle, Peter, Battle Story: *Gallipoli 1915* (The History Press, 2011)

Fosten, D.S.V. & Marrion, R.J., *The German Army 1914–18* (Osprey, 2008)

Gilbert, Martin, *First World War* (HarperCollins, 1994)

Gray, Randal, *Chronicle of the First World War, vols 1 & 2* (Facts on File, 1991)

Hart, Peter, 1918: *A Very British Victory* (Weidenfeld & Nicholson, 2008)

Hart, Peter, *Gallipoli* (Profile Books, 2011)

Hart, Peter, *Somme* (Weidenfeld & Nicolson, 2005)

Haythornthwaite, P.J., *The World War One Source Book* (Arms and Armour Press, 1996)

Horne, Alistair, *The Price of Glory: Verdun 1916* (Penguin, 1993)

Keegan, John, *The First World War* (Hutchinson, 1999)

Middlebrook, Martin, *The First Day on the Somme* (Military Book Society, 1971)

Pope, Stephen & Wheal, Elizabeth-Anne, *The Macmillan Dictionary of the First World War* (Macmillan, 1995)

Root, G. Irving, *Battles East: A History of the Eastern Front of the First World War* (Publish America, 2007)

Steel, Nigel & Hart, Peter, *Passchendaele: The Sacrificial Ground* (Phoenix, 2001)

Stevenson, David, 1914–1918: *The History of the First World War* (Penguin, 2004)

Stone, Norman, *The Eastern Front 1914–1917* (Penguin, 1975)

Stone, Norman, *World War One: A Short History* (Penguin, 2008)

Tuchman, Barbara W., *The Guns of August* (Presidio Press, 2004)

Discover more books in this series ...

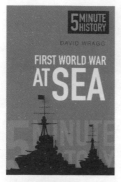

Visit our website and discover thousands
of other History Press books.

www.thehistorypress.co.uk

The
History
Press